Securing Red-The Return of the Republic

For information about custom editions, special sales, and premium and corporate purchases, please contact Matthew Dula at mattdula@gmail.com.

Wrap art designed by: M.R.Dula

About the Author

M.R. Dula was raised in North Carolina as a military brat. He then joined the Marines and spent five years circling the globe and completing two tours overseas. He spends his time helping advance the human condition with his writings, opinions, and patriotism. This manual is his contribution to the future of the country after working as the Strategic Initiatives Director for Trump Victory NC in 2020.

Preface

This book is not designed to target any particular person, event, idea, or effort. It will stay away from negativity and direct targeting. This after action, battle damage assessment, post mortum, or what ever you'd like to call it, was written to help pave the way for future campaigns to learn from the past, adapt to the present, and evolve.

They way Republicans partake in politics reflects greatly on the public perception of the party and further extends to the candidates themselves. Every system requires an assessment and has room for improvement. Political machines are no different. If we only allow natural progression we will be quickly left behind by our competition.

A good portion of our play book was adapted from the left and they have since moved on to new tactics. This book addresses some of the easer ways to improve our political position no matter what position you are in.

2020 was a year full of discovery. We uncovered the true intentions of the communist and socialist agendas that many on the left support. We discovered the strength of the silent majority in the nation. We outed the way technology has been weaponized by corporations against the right.

We also discovered that no matter what the world throws at us we must always take the high road, lead by example and put people first.

Securing Red

The Return Of The Republic

        vi.   Apps

        vii.   Big Data

   b.   Real Time Modeling

        i.   Volunteer Data

        ii.   Metric Tracking

        iii.   Data Up, Data Down

        iv.   Artificial Intelligence

Article IV.   Neighborhood Teams

3.   The new way forward

   a.   Formation

        i.   1:1's and Relationship building

        ii.   Maga Meetups

        iii.   TVLI's

        iv.   Maintenance and Escalation

   b.   Activation

        i.   What to ask and when to ask it

        ii.   Metrics

        iii.   People first, mission always mentality

4.   The On-Ramp

   a.   When the workload increases

        i.   Early campaign

        ii.   Mid Campaign

        ii.   Volunteers
   b.   Integrations
        i.   Higher level coordination
        ii.   Local Candidates
        iii.   Surrogates
   c.   Staffing
        i.   Have the right amount of manpower
        ii.   Roles, Responsibilities, and
Expectations
        iii.   Empowering the volunteer
   d.   Media and Press
        i.   Social Media
        ii.   Press Relations

Article VII.   Strategic Initiatives

8.   Coalitions
   a.   Types
        i.   Major Coalitions
        ii.   Minor Coalitions
        iii.   Volunteer led Coalitions
   b.   Field Integration
        i.   Maximizing small staffs in large states
        ii.   Digital Tools

      iii.   Empowering the Field Organizer

  c.   Surrogates

      i.   Focus on the large turnout

      ii.   Volunteer contact and recruitment

Article VIII. Acts of God (Or China)

9.   When the world shuts down

  a.   Covid

      i.   Emergency Response

      ii.   Plan for the next event

      iii.   Transitioning

      iv.   The Future

  b.   Election Fraud

      i.   Election Integrity Planning

      ii.   Paper Trails

      iii.   Messaging

      iv.   Legal Fights

Article IX.   Securing Red beyond 2020

10. Thoughts on the Future of the party and campaigning

  a.   Security Threats

       i.   Digital

       ii.   Physical

  b.   Reaching outside of our baseline

       i.   Changing the face of the party

       ii.   Inclusion and diversity

  c.   Technology

       i.   The missing piece of the puzzle

  d.   The next generation of leaders

       i.   Younger, Faster, Stronger

       ii.   Understanding new viewpoints

       iii.   Adapting and Evolving

  e.   Last Remarks

"Together, We will make America strong again. We will make wealthy again. We will make America proud again. We will make America safe again. And yes, together, we will make America great again. Thank you. God bless you. And God bless America."

-Donald Trump

Article I.
Machines and Men

What does a modern day campaign look like? When you think about what a Republican, or Democrat, or even a Libertarian modern campaign looks and feels like, what is the first thing that comes to mind? Is it the candidates? The debates? The endless stream of information coming from the mainstream media? How about the constant social media barrage on your timelines and feeds? This question has a very complex answer and in the truth lies an even greater iceberg of complexities.

The modern day Trump Victory campaign is a miracle of machine and man. The seamless integration of digital platforms combined with an army of grassroots on-the-ground teams created the recipe to secure red in 2020 and is what will be used to continue ensuring we win in the future. I would be remiss if I didn't share with how these two processes came together.

Brad Parscale was the digital factor and the book entitled; *Groundbreakers:How Obama's 2.2 Million Volunteers Transformed Campaigning in America*, by Hahrie Han and Elizabeth McKenna, was the physical factor. The entire Trump Victory Campaign in 2020 can be traced back to these two factors. Both of which were in play during the 2016 campaign but interestingly enough would rise to dominance separately of each other in both campaigns.

For anyone who has been paying attention Brad Parscale was the driving force behind the 2016 Trump Campaign in which much of the victory is credited to the direct efforts of hundreds of millions of dollars being poured into digital campaigns including the use of social media giants like FaceBook and Twitter. The scope and nature of what the 2016 campaign was able to accomplish on these platforms will never be matched again.

First, these platforms would prove to become the enemy of free speech with censorship. Customer remorse from the 2016 campaign and the inability to control fake news set in quickly after the 2016 campaign by the tech giants. For our 2020 campaign though, the great social giant that was established in 2016 would not be the same. These issues did drive change though. President Trump would sign the executive order on preventing online censorship on may 28th, 2020 to combat the clampdown of these companies.

Other patriots like Dan Bongino and his partners would go to form social media companies like Parler, which was touted as the Facebook alternative. Even platforms like Youtube and twitter have become places that are no longer safe for your first amendment. This overarching issue is still as prevalent as ever because the tech oligarchs still have free range on your rights until we can amend section 230 and hold them accountable.

In the 2020 election Brad was promoted to Campaign manager and would re-invigorate the 2016 digital strategy. This proved more difficult from my perspective because of the level of resent from the 2016 campaign by the tech giants and the fake news narratives involving Russian interference like the pee-pee tape hoax and the Mueller report and how social media was "weaponized" against the left. Brad was, and still is, a digital media genius. He was able to use the lefts own tools against them and win.

Brad was able to bring a gun to a knife fight in the ally the left paved for us to get ambushed in. The point I am making is that our two party system in America has many battlefields and we won the war of reaching the American people. This was invaluable in

2016, proved it could adapt in 2020, and will need to evolve beyond this last election cycle.

In 2008 the left created a model of political volunteer activation which would later be coined the Neighborhood Team model. This model, used to elect Barrack Hussien Obama, at the time a Senator from Illinois, proved to be extremely adapt at getting normal everyday people to engage in activities that would ultimately drive the vote.

This model was refined by the left in 2012 for President Obama's reelection campaign. The Republican party had not experienced a Presidential win in twelve years by the time Donald Trump decided to and was nominated for the President of the United States. Needless to say, we analyzed it, we studied it, we reverse engineered it and then we build it to suit our party, our values, and our way of campaigning. Then we deployed it.

These two forces are the greatest influences on the successful election and reelection of the most needed president since George Washington. Independently they are extremely powerful but combined they proved to be able to not only ensure Donald Trump's victory but combat some of the highest level of corruption, collusion, conspiracy and content the left and it's army of corporate traitors could through at us.

III. Physical

The organizational model for the 2016 and 2020 campaign is the Neighborhood Team Model. This model involves staff members in command and control roles while compartmentalizing specific roles and tasks among the volunteers that are recruited. Regional Field Directors would control Field Organizers within various turfs in a state and those FO's would then control neighborhood team leaders. These NTL's would then in turn control Core Team Members who would then control the actions of the boot on the ground volunteer.

This model is directly taken from the lefts play book. It was then adapted and retooled for the our utilization with much success and some failure. This model requires very strong leaders up and down the chain to maximize effectiveness. The ability to make real time decisions on the ground as well as from a higher level leadership perspective is critical and requires strong levelheaded leaders.

One of the most important first steps with this

model and within any organization, paid or volunteer, is RRE's, or: Roles, responsibilities, and expectations. Every single person within the organization needs to know their role. This could boil down to a job description but it must be very explicit. The same should be done for responsibilities. Within a campaign your RRE's might change from the beginning of the campaign to something completely different in the the last 50 days. This is why it is critical that they are outlined and when they change they are updated for your troops. This will help remove confusion on the battlefield of the campaign and keep your employees and volunteers focused.

Clear cut communication from the beginning will save you so much headache and time as you begin to increase your goals and workload. Having an employee that doesn't understand why work production continually increases and his RRE's are changing weekly is going to cripple your production. Outlining responsibilities early will help staff and volunteers prepare for the whirlwind of 18-20 hour a day schedules as you get the to the final stretch.

Operational security is a huge hole in our current political landscape. Look no further than Hillary Clinton's email server fiasco. Granted, I am very glad those pieces of evidence are out in the public, but it goes to show that without proper planning and attention to detail the little things become huge problems down stream. Our party needs to focus on physical security and threat mitigation training at our locations, for our rallies, for our Maga meetups and in person events. The left has radicalized with Antifa and BLM protests which will pick back up every election cycle. The violence or threat of violence is not going away. Communism does not sleep. We must ensure we take care of our people.

One up, one down. This is a term used to describe that any given employee should know how to do the job of the person below them and above them. This training will prove invaluable as the cycle comes to the end. When you can have the trust and the faith in an employee to be able to stay fluid and flexible through an event or task that is not a primary function or RRE it will make your life so much easier and the machine will run smoother overall.

Campaigning is stressful. It is long hours, people facing, pressure mounting, no holds bare work. It can be physically, mentally, and morally demanding if you are not prepared. It can also be the seed of destruction within the organization if stress is not managed correctly. Morale and Welfare are concepts of taking care of your staff, your volunteers, and anyone who you come in contact with to do your job. As a leader you must always remember that even the smallest foreign concept like a close poll or increased metric of production can take the wind out of the sails of your people.

You must combat that stress and pressure with addressing the need of your people. Ensure they are taking care of their bodies, minds, families, and personal business. Demand a work life balance even if they don't think they can have one. You make time for the things you care about don't you? Make them care about one another and themselves and you will have steady production and happier staff. Find what motivates your staff and volunteers and make a point of including that in routines surrounding welfare and morale.

One of the best ways to stress test the systems and organizational models your going to employ over the cycle is to "sandbox." This term comes from big tech but it's applications know no boundaries of industry. Sandboxing is the purposeful establishment of a test environment in which winning and losing carry no cost to the organization. You are free to develop, test, deploy, and change the parameters of the inputs without expending precious resources.

This is by far the best way to test various components and people of the organization within any given part of the cycle without spending money and more importantly time. As the cycle draws closer to the end you are forced to make choices that close out other options. An example would be having to chose using money, people, or time to solve a problem. Testing these scenarios out in sandbox mode can help you see the right answers when the time comes. There are many tools available to do this but the fastest will be to set aside time upfront during the campaign.

Campaigns, just like any actual free money market business, need to be extremely organized and experts at communication. This is where we need to do better about following in our Trumps footsteps and adapting a more robust business model and implementing it quickly. Campaigns run on people. Those people do not need to guess as to who is in charge, who does what, and how this system is suppose to run.

Every campaign going forward needs to immediately establish company organization charts that outline every position, who reports to whom, and what every division and subset looks like. No matter who holds the title within the box every person within the campaign will know exactly who is doing what and where they belong within the organization. This will establish a chain of command and having that will make communications smoother, faster, and less messy.

Another extremely important aspect of campaigning that needs to be adjusted is Human Resources. HR is one of the most critical components of any company or campaign. Without the right HR division a campaign is going to suffer greatly. Ensuring we are hiring the right people for our staff, handling the day to day issues that arise from normal operations, and all the way to firing are critical to mitigate risk, liability, and lawsuits.

Without the proper staff ensuring human resource issues are taken care of legally and appropriately the campaign will be stuck in a *"what we hire is what we get"* cycle. This is very damaging because if we had taken the time to hire the right candidates to do things like field organizing all the way to our directors we could be more efficient long term. Campaign culture matters.

III. Digital

As mentioned earlier the digital part of campaigning has become a bedrock of success. The most critical player is data. Data rules the world. It should be the entire point of any digital campaign. Without it you will always be in the dark. The RNC spent millions of dollars on data and created one of the smartest long term systems which is a data center. This treasure trove needs fine tooth combing and constant testing and updating. Without ensuring the data is accurate and timely it will quickly be a waste of money and resources.

This is were digital tool integration comes into play. Tools like phone dialers, door knocking apps, surveys, newsletters, social media, text alerts, and every other tool we use needs to all conduct one main goal. Feed the data center with new information. We live in a fake news cycle world along with main stream media being more divided and because of that we can no longer rely on third party unbiased assessments and analysis. We need to control and account for our own success and failures. Content is king and we need to own our content and the content of our efforts.

Our digital win in 2016 jump started a political campaign upheaval the likes of which we have yet to completely understand or even comprehend. The GOP, The RNC, and Republicans everywhere will need to start all playing from the same sheet of music for the next election cycle. Big data is going to be the joint operations center for this. Currently, from at least my own observation, the state Trump Victory campaign had a very hard time integrating into the long standing GOPs at the county level. This cost use very dearly. When we have multiple campaign efforts that are not coordinating efforts and resources we end up with more mess and less results. Using data we can in the future explain why it is of the utmost importance to work as fully integrated partners in the future.

This also means we need to explore new ideas about our application of technology. If data is what we seek we need to solve the problem of integration. I am a huge fan of competition but we must consolidate our ways of using our digital tools. Having multiple contracts with multiple partners for phone banking apps or door knocking or taking surveys or what ever we are doing for voter contact needs to be owned by the RNC. They need to spend the money to develop the apps to match the data center so we own every part of the chain.

It will be cheaper in the long run to own the data and the input apps and devices than to spend millions on other companies products and lose the data or not retain ownership of information. We also loose productivity when we have to rely on these partners to make adjustments or when their systems go down. Owning control of the tools will ensure we have them available when we need them, streamline issues as they arise, and increase the capability to scale down from the national level to the volunteer on the ground.

We must keep pace with the technological revelations around us. This means looking into the future and planning backwards. What will campaigning look like in 20 years? How will it be conducted? What can the last 20 years teach us about the pace of adoption and implementation? What lessons can we learn now and forecast or project that will be expensive or painful in the future?

We must develop a single source campaign platform that allows for seamless physical use. If we plan on evolving with our world and the way in which we use tech we must dream again. We are a mobile world and one of the biggest lessons of 2020 is that we can not afford to lose ground to challenges like a world wide pandemic.

The China virus halted all in person efforts around the nation. The entire world shifted to digital platforms. This lesson must not be lost on us. We need a single platform app build around our data center that handles all of our needs. From securing our documents to handling our emails and knocking doors to phone banking we need a single, secure, platform.

This platform needs to be modular, adaptable, and scalable to all our needs nationwide and so easy to use any volunteer can set an account up and start activating. Having multiple layers and account parameters to allow for senior staff nationally, statewide, and staff while being user friendly for any volunteer. We must also account for artificial intelligence in our future. The data we collect and use should be carefully modeled in quantum time to present multiple options during sandbox and in live campaign scenarios.

IV. Neighborhood Teams

The neighborhood team model is the most

powerful method of organizing the grassroots efforts ever conceived. This method is able to collect the lowest common denominator together for activation despite geographical or financial hurdles. The Trump campaign understood the power that was demonstrated by this model during the Obama cycles. This model would be fielded during the 2016 campaign and then further refined and honed for the 2020 cycle.

The key to the neighborhood teams are relationships. Real relationships. What is the end goal of any campaign? To Win, Decisively. To beat the opponent and become the elected official in which you are running for. This requires votes. These votes are not just numbers at the end of a tally. They are actual humans with feeling, wants, desires, fears, and choice. The neighborhood team model allows for the highest level of building real and valuable relationships with the actual voter.

This is done by the field organizer. This is where all of the proper campaign formation, organization, and most importantly human resources comes into play. You can hire anyone for this position but you would be doing a disservice to the cycle. If the entire physical campaign revolves around the relationships that FO's build with volunteers it would be wise to make sure these employees are of a very high quality and caliber.

I am under no illusion that resources, time constraints, and talent pools for remote locations can factor into how this is carried out, but the most effective teams have great FO's. Strong leadership qualities, great interpersonal relationship skills, lock tight time management skills along with drive and initiative are all required.

The FO has many tools available to effectively build these teams. The most important of these is the one on one. This is the moment in which the FO can spend some quality time investigating and ascertaining the potential downstream kinetic energy of a person. The ultimate goal is to find and recruit volunteers who are well rounded and capable of not only activating to do certain things like door knock and make calls but also recruit others.

The zest needed to do this, and be capable of finding others to do this with you, is what makes great neighborhood team leaders. To bring together your small group of NTLs and open the pipeline up for greater engagement driven social events need to be conducted. It's not secret that the Trump Campaign was an expert at the MAGA Meetup. These highly social and rewarding experiences would bring together many like minded individuals and ultimately prove to be the fertile ground needed to start a serious recruitment and activation campaign early in the cycle.

It's not enough to just gather and express our support of a candidate though. Once your social meetings conclude the real work starts. This is the bread and butter of the FO. Contacting and escalating the new participants in the neighborhood team.

I can not stress enough how powerful an actual phone call is. Our high tech world is full of ways to reach out to people. Social media, texts, emails, etc. have made communication impossible to hide from now. But, these methods are hard to make personal. To truly build that relationship which is the glue that will keep the zest in the volunteer you must call them. I don't care if they don't answer. Leave a message. Your voice will pierce the veil of excuses and spark connections that will lead to activation.

All of this will lead to training sessions on different aspects of the campaign. These sessions will help train many volunteers on critical issues like how to use door knocking apps, phone banking, campaign organization and activation initiatives and any other critical information the campaign needs to share.

These sessions are were the FO steps into that leadership role and assigns tasks and responsibility directly to the volunteers. This creates a dynamic of hierarchy and command and control to the actions of volunteers. What good is it to have 60 volunteers if they all do different things every week? They need to all be focused on very specific goals. This only happens if failure is a removed and replaced.

Failing to help the candidate, failing to help the neighborhood, failing to keep their end of the bargain. This failure must be balanced with reward. Volunteers are giving up so much to do the things they do for us. We must remember that. They are not paid, they don't get compensated. They are doing it because they believe and they have zest. We must reinforce those beliefs and reward the zest. Set up a system of positive reenforcement after specific actions are completed. Make an extra special phone call to a great volunteer. Send them a campaign shirt or hat as a reward for efforts above the baseline. Submit them to VIP lists and special campaign calls if they prove themselves. Show them why they are valuable to the team and then ask more of them.

How do you get someone who isn't getting paid anything to do something they might now normally do? By knowing how and when to ask. This is a critical component of building those relationships with your volunteers. What internal or external motivators does that volunteer have? What issues do they care about? What time do you know they have to dedicate to campaign activities? These are all items of inventory you need to conduct with each volunteer and enter into a CRM or database to best leverage any situation.

You have two eyes, two ears, and 1 mouth. That is a 4:1 ratio of listening to speaking. If you practice this ratio you will see or hear what will need to be said to get the yes. That yes is expensive though. It will require time, patience, and a willingness to invest. Diversify your investments into people and you will see growth within your teams. Don't ever stop at the first yes. If you get a no start the inventory process over again. Default back to the 4:1 ratio. Do this until you get the yes but be smart about it. Update your CRM and wait for the right time to circle back. Everyone has a yes button. Be patient and persistent, take inventory, use the 4:1 ratio and when the time presents itself, slam that yes button. Lock them in and the continue to ask them for more to keep them engaged. Idle volunteers will fall off quick.

When we get into the work of actually campaigning we think of things like phone banking, door knocking, social posts, meetups, voter registrations and many other activities. All of these activities need to be crafted in a way that is calculated and captured. If it is decided that every volunteer needs to knock 100 doors a day we must ensure we are explaining why. Why is the metric this way? Why are these particular efforts the most important thing to focus on right now? If we do not communicate effectively with our volunteers and staff we will lose them to poor morale.

The difference maker is knowledge. When someone knows why they are performing an astronomically important task and the future impacts of not completing them they buy in. We need this buy in with everything we ask. We must leverage the zest, get the buy in, and then the ask seems doable. Lead like this, *"People first, Mission always"*. Put our volunteers first but always complete the mission.

Campaigns, as complex and fast paced as they are, can be easily graphed as an exponent. The closer you get to the election date the faster and higher that graph rises. Each election will be different as to how fast this line rises but you will find an on ramp. This is the point in which the workload starts to increase, the metrics rise, and production becomes the focus. Until you reach the on ramp you need to focus everything on ensuring that when you do meet the on ramp you are ready for the ride after you get on the campaign super highway. There are very distinct paces between early in the campaign, the middle and the end of the cycle.

Focus on building up as much of your end requirements before you get on the ramp. This means establishing your organization, your teams, your social and digital platforms early and in full. As you get to the end you lose the time to build things and even small things like losing just one volunteer can put huge ripples in your systems. If you only had a half staff of volunteers, the phone goal is 200 calls a day, and one quits; then everyone else is highly effected by that ripple and the workload increases while morale lowers. Setting up your systems of production and leveraging the proper tools will help reduce the drag associated with small changes within your neighborhood teams.

For the 2020 campaign the final quarter was the

last 50 days. This is when you no longer can spend your time building and testing. It is game time. The buzzer is going to sound soon and you need to put every resource into the ensuring the win. You are not going to have much time to do anything else but get those votes. It is critical that this is what you plan and build for. When you know the date of the dance you can prepare the best card in advance.

V. Timelines

It was a real shock to me when I learned that even though we knew when all of our efforts would be tabulated into a crescendo of success we did not plan that way. In any organization, when you know what is needed to be done by when, such as a major project or a specific contract, you usually always reverse plan for it. This was a critical component of the the campaign in which I wish was carried out. Had we had a plan from November 3rd backwards we could have not only executed a step-by-step manual but we could have measured everything. Real time data and feedback loops could help us plot micro and macro movements, swings, needs, and requirements throughout the campaign.

Now, for those who actually campaign you are probably saying, "There is just so much we can't plan for. Events, surrogates, polls, activation requirements, etc..". I call bullshit. I'm not saying we need to plan every single detail and not deviate. I'm saying we need to create overlapping calenders that are fluid in nature but are built to carry out a very specific need. The need to win. If we know how many voters we need to register, contact, activate, and get to the polls to actually vote we can and should reverse engineer the campaign to start our efforts off with the highest statistical probability of success.

This planning needs to envelope every aspect of the campaign. Everything from how much money we need donated to what is the optimal time for a volunteer to knock a door or make a call. Combine this with a single source campaign app and we should be able to complete the feedback loop to assess in real time what needs to be tweaked. We must stop playing checkers with campaigning and start playing quantum chess.

All of this requires a base camp and integrations. The base camp of the RNC should be responsible for the data and the platforms. Higher level integration would be from the party candidate campaign and lower level integration would come from the state and local GOPs and local candidates. There will most likely always be campaign finance issues, a maze of legal conundrums, and operational challenges but if we can navigate these with this model in mind we will light years ahead of the competition. This was almost realized in the 2020 cycle. The RNC paid millions for a data center but struggled to be the base camp and bridge between the state and national level campaigns. they need to devote more resources to engineer a solid base camp that creates a seamless and fluid system.

A system that allows for two way communication and operational oversight covering the highest and lowest levels of joint campaign organizations would ensure all activities that need to be conducted are smooth and timelines are effective. In North Carolina it proved hard to get many local GOPs to concentrate efforts and integrate with the Trump Victory Campaigns. Political infighting, lack of leadership, poor planning, volunteer positions, resource waste, and overlapping efforts led to at best times of chaos. The local pulse was hyper focused on the small candidate campaigns with higher level presidential efforts or requests being put low in the stack of things to get done.

We must make sure they understand that integrating and working together will ensure an entire ballot win. From the top all the way down. We must figure out how to reunite the party, remove divisional differences, and become one fighting and campaigning unit again.

All of these efforts will ensure that when we must activate our timelines and campaign plans that we work as one unit. *One team, One Fight*. The same way we look after our volunteers, the same way we lead them, ensure they are taken care of, the rewards and the enhancements are needed throughout our country. If we are truly only a two party system then we must become the best. This will only occur if we can unite our party under great leaders and empowering tools. People run campaigns and people elect our officials.

This leads to how all of these overlapping systems and timelines need to unite. Depending on who is running for the presidential ticket, what candidates are running for Republican slots and local candidates will vastly affect how easy it will be to work them into a reverse timeline. The RNC and the county GOPs will also factor into the overall timeline.

One of the interesting takeaways from this cycle is learning that almost none of these cogs works together or they have a very hard time integrating with each other. The local GOP chapters are OFP (Own Fucking Program), the congressional and senate campaigns have campaigns built on what has worked and are hard to test the waters are bring on new ways of conducting business for fear of losing and the RNC seems to only drop in every two to four years or when a particular candidate is critical to the overall national Republican strategy.

This means all of our calenders and efforts are out of sync and even worse could mean that the actual grunt work could be wasting resources that could have been saved if they were coordinating. We need to solve the problem of command and control and make sure all parties and candidates have a system to fall in-line behind. If we can produce this model we will sync everyone up and down the ballot behind a monster machine. This will ease our timelines across the board and make all of our efforts maximize production and outcome. This big data, big picture model will carry us forward from 2020 into the next decade of campaigning.

VI. Events

Every campaign needs events. These are the bread and butter of getting the constituents together to rub elbows, share policy, cut deals, recruit volunteers, raise money, and bring the message home. Unfortunately, these are not easy to pull off. We have all been to horrible events. They can actually work to hurt a candidate, alienate a base, stifle monetary support, and persuade a voter away.

On the other hand we have all been to great events. Some events leave the participant with a sense of awe and grandeur of a candidate that can spark a fervor within them to get involved, donate money and open doors. The Trump Campaign has mastered the later. A hallmark of the 2016 and carried into the 2020 campaign is the Rally. Presidential rallies are one music set short of a rock concert. Even some state candidate events in 2020 could classify as sensational mass events.

Regardless if you are a local candidate or working on presidential campaigns it is critical to ensure you have great events. This all comes down to planning and communication. *No one plans to fail, they fail to plan.* The number one thing you have to ask is, "who owns the event?" This little question will help you answer many of the follow on aspects that arise from ensuring success.

If you can afford it you need to hire people into the campaign who have event planning backgrounds. This smart hire will save you mountains of money and time as you try to put together events that lead to conversions. Event coordinators have the skill set and the tools to make sure all the details are attended too. Without them, you will struggle to make sure every aspect of your events are solid.

This might not seem like it is important but when you start factoring in how tightly controlled some of the details are within an event and how much detail actually goes into an event you will quickly realize professional help is required. Having the right manpower for your events will elevate your events quickly as the "Must-Go" events within the campaign and lead to faster results.

This professional must also be a strong leader. Many campaign strategies require a massive amount of delegation of duties. This could be because of a financial limitation, time limitation, or geographical issue. Many campaigns will create the master plan and issue orders to volunteers or lower level employees to ensure the staffing requirements are taken care of. This is a very smart way in creating inclusion within the staff and volunteer ranks but it must be carefully balanced with communication. There is nothing more stressful then working with an advanced team from a higher level or a state level coordinator and not having all the info.

Most events that come down the pipe to you will have an advanced team, a security team, a state team and a local team integration that needs to work seamlessly. This is all usually stressed by the very small amount of time to get it set up. The majority of events are pulled off with a week of less of planning. A high percentage of events have even less time. This means that the highest on the totem pole usually gets the least amount of information. Having a strong events coordinator that can outline roles, responsibilities, and expectations along with timelines to all parties will make the event a success or not.

This level of coordination is not easy. Working with other campaigns or even different levels within your own campaign can be frustrating at best. The fastest way to overcome this is to pick the phone up and call the point of contacts. Emails are sloppy and one way communication channels. After you get someone on the phone follow up with an email outlining everything that was talked about and then move forward. This direct communication method is the oldest and still the best at forcing all parties to coordinate.

Once the ball gets rolling RRE's need to be handed out immediately. This allows all levels to get on the same sheet of music quickly and ensures all calenders are locked in. Local candidates usually cherry pick the best events to attend or partake in and you want to make sure they are on locked in.

These events need some horsepower to make sure they become the talking point in an attendees future interactions. This horsepower is extremely expensive if you are hiring for each event. That is were your volunteers come in to play. Some events like the MAGA Rallies required eighty to a hundred volunteers to pull them off successfully. That is a huge amount of manpower that needs to be planned for and controlled on scene. You must ensure that the volunteer finishes an event with a sense of accomplishment, duty, and fulfillment. If they don't, you won't see them again on your volunteer rosters. Make sure your volunteers know as much information as humanly possible. Think of each event as a rock concert that needs a complete production and director. They need to know when to show up, what to wear, weather concerns, roles, responsibilities, expectations, and how they work in the bigger machine.

I have seen some great volunteers and some horrible ones. The difference is usually you as the event coordinator. People who are not getting paid and have volunteered there time and resources to help you out require the extra effort to ensure they are happy and will answer your call the next time. Empower your volunteers and you will have great events.

You no doubt will want to ensure that your event is covered by some form of media. Whether that is traditional media sources like Fox or local news channels to independent journalists and social media influencers you need to have a plan to deal with them. Press tents, media credentials, and preplanned press locations within your event make handling press a smooth operation.

VII. Strategic Initiatives

Strategic Initiatives is a relatively new concept

for Republicans. Traditional campaigning has meant appealing to the base and moving on. Strategic Initiatives (SI) is the act of creating coalitions around voters that might not be traditionally within your base. This means that you should be setting up coalitions to focus on voters based on factors like religion, industries of work, ethnicities, and interests. Coalitions like Veterans, Black Voices, Catholics, Cops, etc. need to be investigated as potential avenues to find more voters and tailor your messaging and get feedback from potential voters that might be lost in the main sea of your base.

Depending on the size of your campaign you might be limited by resources, people, or money to create and maintain great coalitions ran and controlled by the actual campaign. This is were you can empower volunteers to lead coalitions for your campaign. This also is a great way to put a familiar face to the coalition rather than just you who will most likely not be the right face for that coalition. As a male I know that I am the worst face to be for a womans coalition. Volunteer led coalitions will help spur natural growth and activation.

These coalitions need to be plugged into the main campaign strategy. SI is usually the red headed step child within a campaign because they are so specific and the challenges and issues are not usually synced with main campaign integrations. This is why your coalition coordinators need to have weekly meetings with your directors and field teams. This will allow them to help push or pull resources where they are needed for the main campaign strategies. That can provide tremendous pressure relief during your last days within the campaign.

SI is also usually a very small unit with the campaign. Sometimes it might be one person or just the main manager. If you find yourself in that position you need to leverage the volunteer led coalitions. If you ignore coalition work you are missing out on massive voter pools who might be interested in your campaign and message but traditionally have never even been approached.

This means that you need to make sure your digital tools and social media campaigns are lock tight and correctly delegated out to your coalition coordinators. Using scheduling software and Google shared calenders will save you headache and ensure proper content drip. Everything needs to be issued from the top but controlled by the lowest rung in the chain.

Another great way to maximize your coalitions to comb your existing base of volunteers and start involving them in coalitions you have built or will soon. They are already involved and have buy in and are more willing to step up into leadership roles. It also allows for faster coalition building because they are plugged into the coalition you are looking to build. This work should be put on the field organizers to help sort out and record in the CRM so you can scale quickly.

These coalitions will grow to a size in which you can enact the same tactics used in the neighborhood team models to retain and engage members. This means that you will probably have coalition events as well. One of the best ways to ensure a great event is to have great surrogates. These pre screened and hand picked individuals will help maximize the impact of your time and resources as well as the call to actions you want delivered.

Make sure you set your surrogates up well in advance and they understand what being a surrogate means. They will help make sure you have larger turnouts and a higher likelihood of volunteer engagement. All events in person or digital need to focus on volunteer contact and recruitment. So, if you through a in person meet and greet with a candidate and surrogate you need to make sure you have volunteer signup sheets, a call to action for after the attendees leave and potentially a volunteer action before or after the event like a phone bank or door knocking. This will help you test, verify and discover new volunteers.

VIII. Acts of God (or China)

2020 brought us Covid-19 aka Corona Virus aka China Virus. I don't need to devote much time on the politics of the virus, the global shutdowns, the infringement of our rights, the maskholes, and everything else we have all just lived through. What I will focus on is how a worldwide "Pandemic" changed political campaigns forever.

When the world went into shutdown mode in April of 2020 the Trump Campaign was just in build phase. This meant that when we should have been spending 80% or more of our time conducting in person recruiting and social events we were forced down to 0%. Our entire organization had to switch to a entire virtual campaign conducted off zoom and social media. There wasn't many companies on the planet who were ready for this transition let alone many individuals. The "New Normal" shifted the entire ideology of work, socializing, campaigning, and politics. Our organization struggled tremendously to switch to this new way of productivity.

This is something we need to learn from and never forget. The "New Normal" is here to stay and virtual platforms for campaigns will always be apart of the planning now. This means that all campaigns need to create or at least write a plan for the next medical crisis. All campaigns need to put a medical doctor on staff or at least on retainer to provide guidance on how to navigate the current Covid issues and any future issues that might arise. This will provide a campaign with the ability to immediately issue proper advise to the staff and volunteers that are in line with medical recommendations needed for the situation.

This strategy allows a campaign to stay fluid and productive regardless of what happens in the world. We lost at least 3 months in the campaign were we had no real guidance or advice on how to proceed forward because we were not ready for a pandemic. If we build a medical director spot in campaigns we will be able to stay ahead of the chaos. This role will be worth all the salt it costs when as the country or state shutdown the campaign, under the guidance of it's own internal medical director can coordinate with the other divisions and outline a path forward for the campaign that protects the employees, volunteers and productivity.

Covid also brought to the surface our enemies tactics and plans. Communism and socialism are very real ideologies in America that wish to take everything from us and remove the republic. This was outlined during the push for mail in ballots. Many states implemented mail in ballot laws that were not designed to handle the amount of people who chose to do this over in person voting because of Covid. This means that mail in balloting was ripe for fraud.

This fraud was eventually discovered in multiple states despite what the main stream fraudsters pushed on your news feed. Every campaign from now on needs to have an election integrity division. This division needs to solely focus on how the elections are carried out in that state as well as any and all parties connected to it. Each state has different laws pertaining to 3rd party contracts, voter machines, laws, and processes. This division needs to know how are votes counted, who counts them, what companies have the contracts, where to the ballots come from, who makes them, and how does the process work when there is a challenge or fraud is detected.

We are watching our country be stolen from us one fraudulent ballot at a time and we need to get in front of this. It isn't enough anymore to bring the voters out. We must ensure the legal votes are counted and we aren't being cheated out of our rights and freedoms. We need to demand legislation that creates paper trails, auditable and transparent regulations, and quick closures to when things go wrong. Until those are passed it will be on the campaign and the citizens to ensure election integrity. When all else fails sue, sue, and sue. Legal fights can help build cases, expose information, make people talk, discover fraud, and resolve issues in the favor of the people. It is expense so make sure you have earmarked funds for the legal fights.

IX. Securing Red Beyond 2020

Trump changed the Republican party for good.

he single handedly made the party fraction into those for the people and the republic and those against it. This means that within the last 4 years we learned who in the party was a rhino, who was only in it for themselves, and who really cares about our country. The sad truth is that the last group is very small.

The Republican party must shed the dead weight of selfish elected officials and focus on the founding fathers and our founding documents intent for our country. This also means that Trump changed how campaigns are conducted. The amount of energy, money, and resources need to duplicate what Trump did in 2016 and 2020 might not be matched for another 50 years but we need to try. The model outlined by the Trump team and campaign is the shining example of how a candidate needs to campaign. All candidates need to strive to prove they are going to work on the behalf of the American people and not themselves or foreign interests. America first.

In order to do this we need to harden our country and our campaigns to security threats both digitally and physically. Our hyper connected world makes it too easy to hack an email, steal voter data, or sabotage a campaign. We need to ensure we don't compromise our integrity or the integrity of our nation by getting in bed with Chinese spies or working with communist parties abroad. Pictures of a Vice President's son sleeping with Chinese hookers while flying around on Air force 1 are not good looks for anyone let alone a party.

Campaigns must also realize that elections needs voters. Voters come in all shapes, colors, sizes, sexual orientations, denominations, and viewpoints. We must reach outside of our baselines to understand the voters and ensure we tailor our messaging to help educate them on why our candidate is the right choice and how to actually make that choice on game day. The face of the Republican party is changing and it needs to continue to change. The Democrats believe they own certain ethnicities and demographs. We need to show those groups why they need to wake up and move to the party that will ensure the rights of all Americans.

The future will be controlled by data. That data needs to be owned, maintained, and protected by us, not 3rd parties. We must develop our own technologies, applications, and hubs for to control our data and make our mission easier. This is the missing piece of the puzzle right now. When we fight it by creating this system we will leapfrog our competition.

The republican party should also set up a committee to start identifying the leaders of the future. We must start finding and recruiting good men and woman who are patriots and willing to put country over politics and money. This committee needs to create programs and pathways that breed the next generation of not only Republicans but also our representatives, Congressmen, Senators, and Presidents. Why do we wait around until the last minute to decide who we need to put on the ballots? We should have a dozen highly groomed and qualified choices lined up and ready to go. These leaders will be younger, faster and stronger than those of the past and they will bring new ideas and viewpoints to the party. This growth is necessary and it can be aligned with our traditions and values. We must learn to adapt and evolve with the newer generations not shun them and push them aside.

This manual is not very long and I could spend hundreds of pages on each issue but that isn't my intent. I want anyone reading this to understand that you can't stop time and as every hand of the clock continues forward change marches right along with it. In order for our country to stay in alignment with our founding ideas of individual freedoms, rights, and protections we must get in line with that change. We need to take the time now to set up the next fifty years of the Republican party maintaining control and fending off corruption and communism. Securing Red will require all of us to constantly assess our progress and make the changes necessary to stay on course and return to our Republic.

www.ingramcontent.com/pod-product-compliance
Lightning Source LLC
Chambersburg PA
CBHW041108280526
45792CB00010B/2344